A Dog Can

by Vaishali Batra

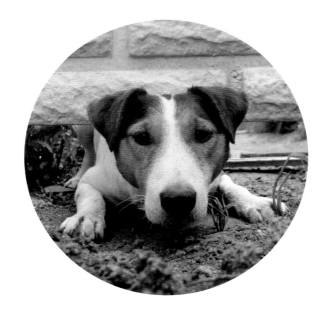

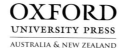

OXFORD
UNIVERSITY PRESS
AUSTRALIA & NEW ZEALAND

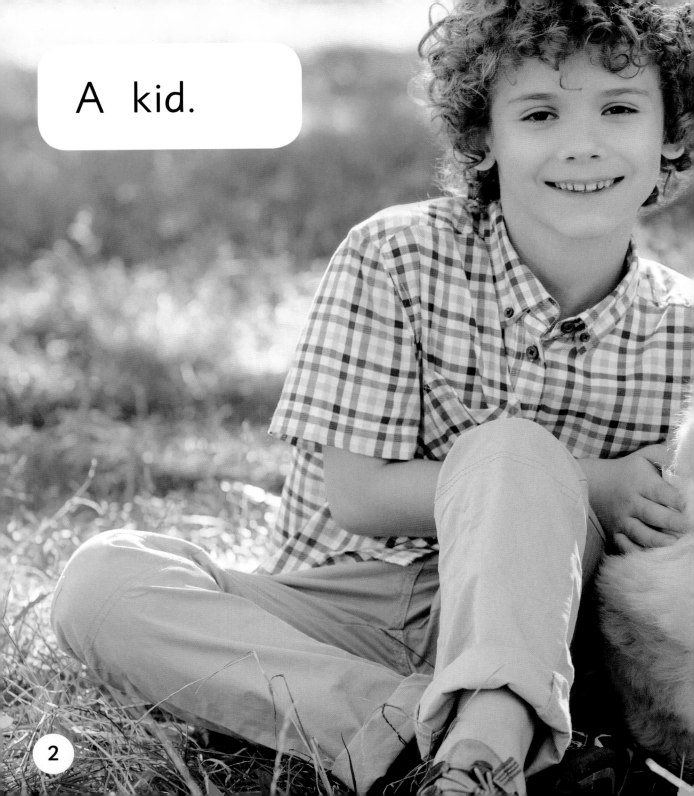

A kid.

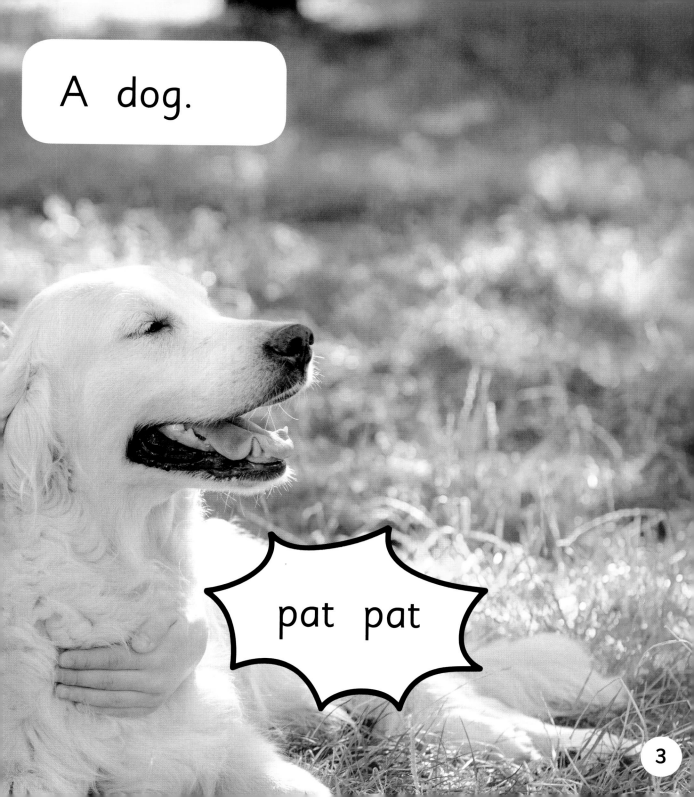

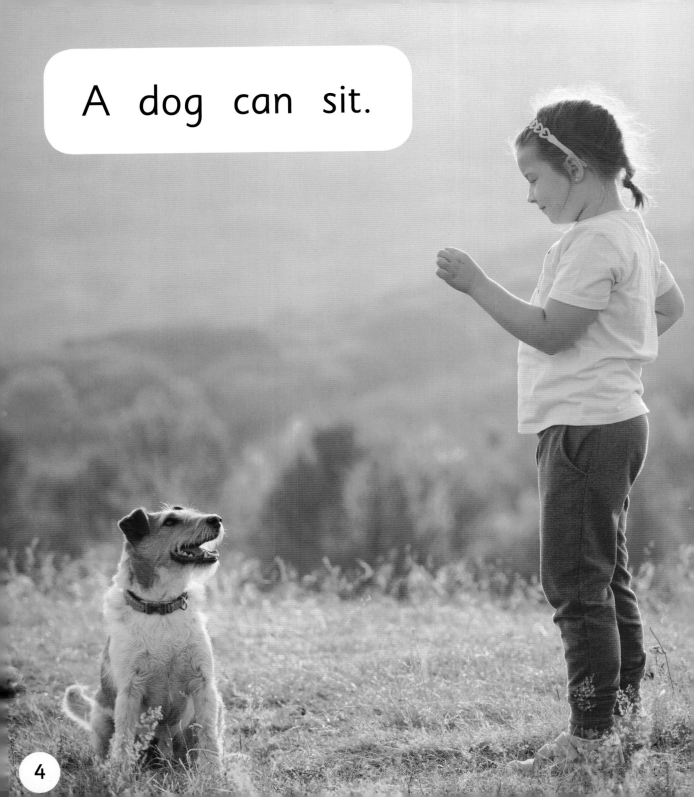

A dog can sit.

It is on top.

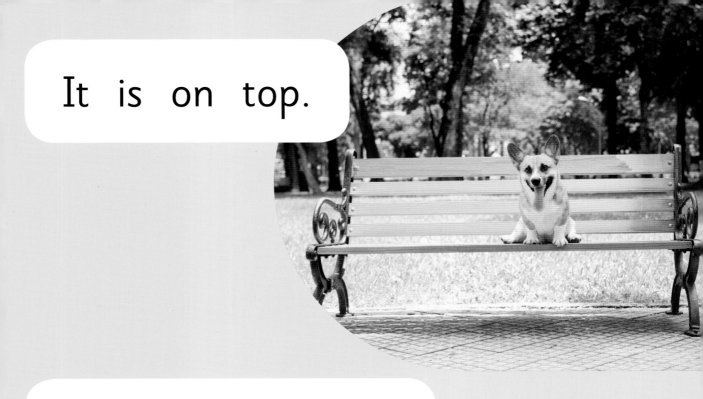

It is not on top.

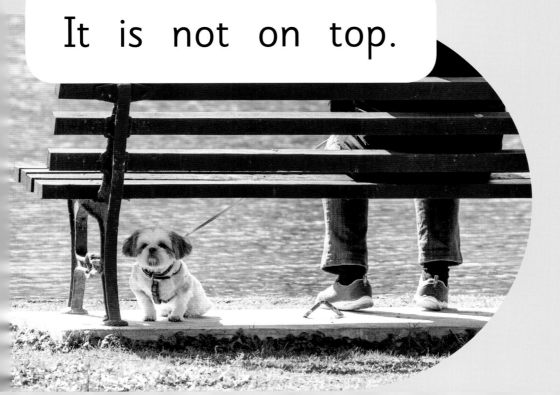

A dog can sip.

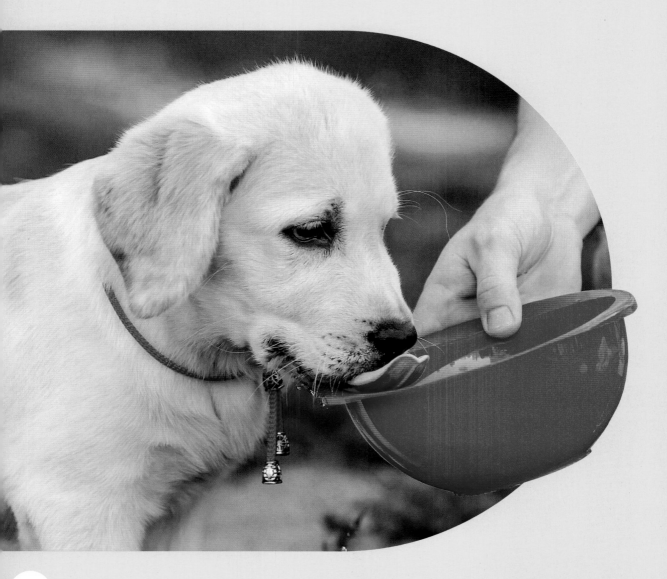

It can tip it.

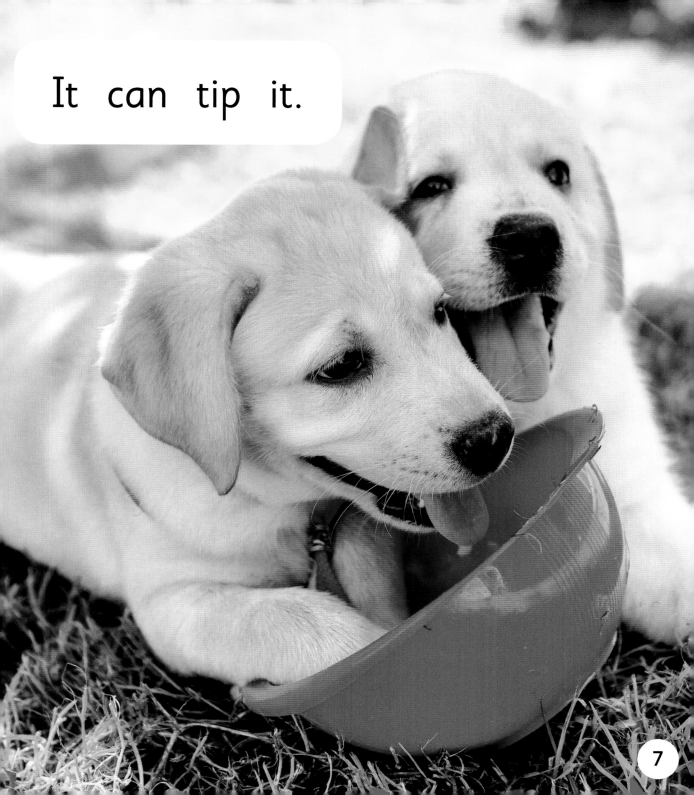

A dog can dig.

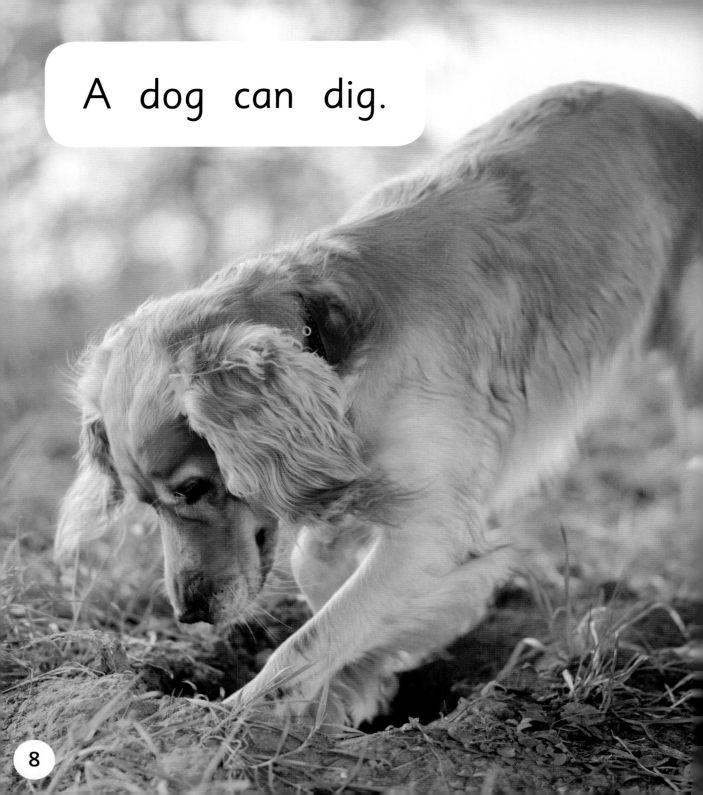

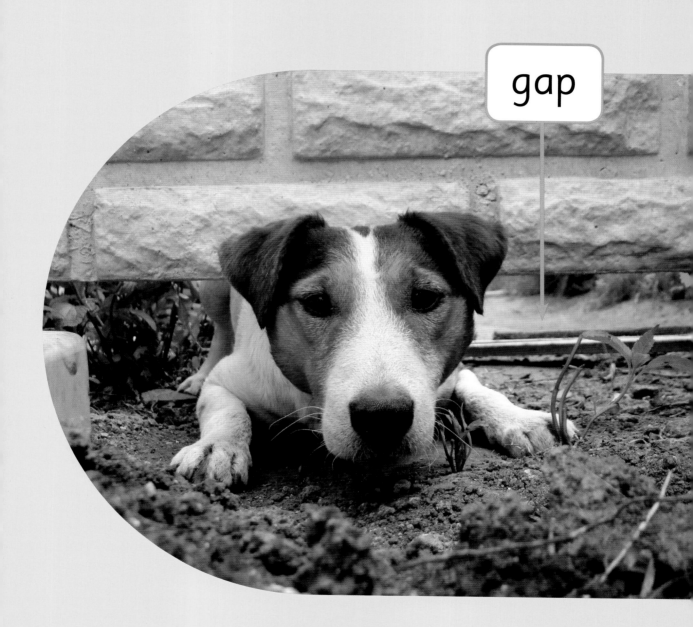

gap

A dog got a mat.

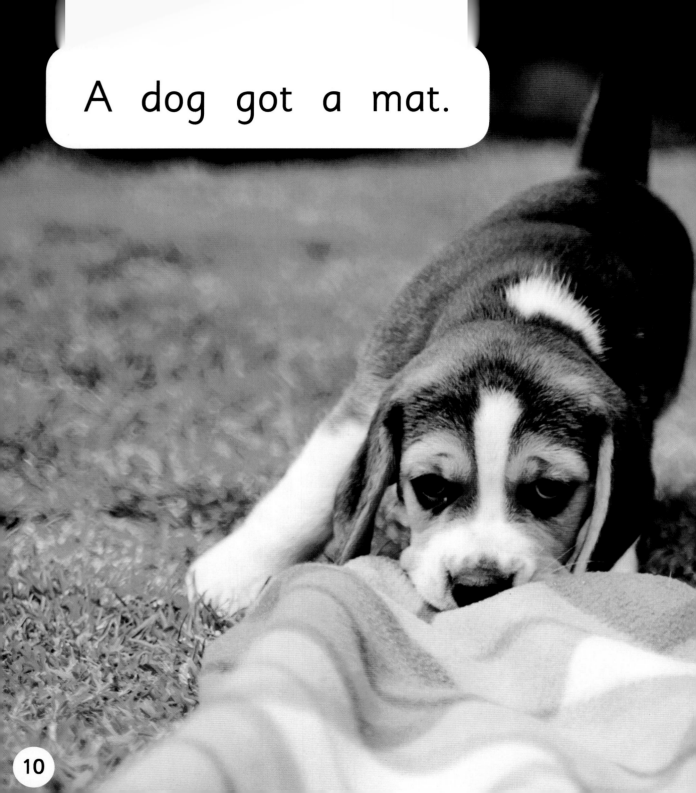

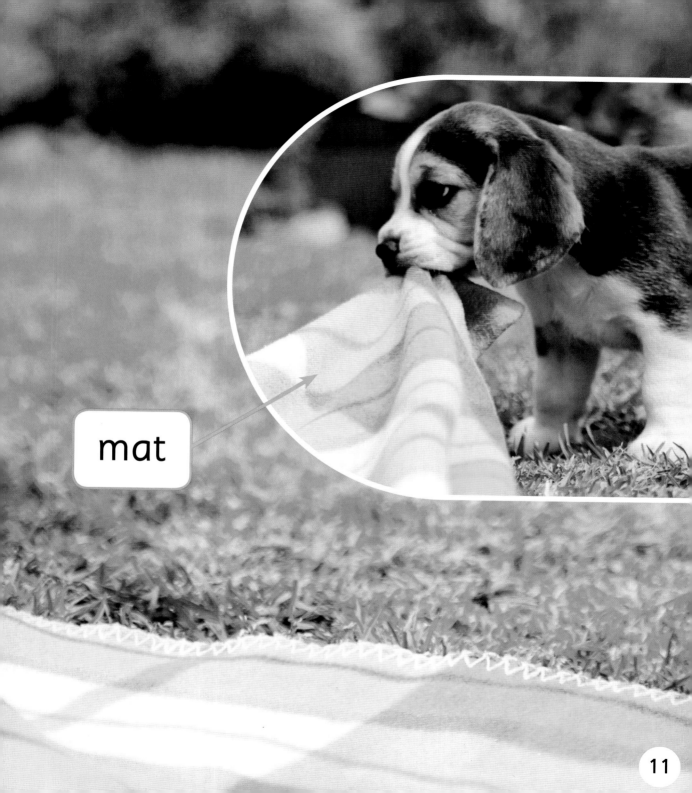

mat

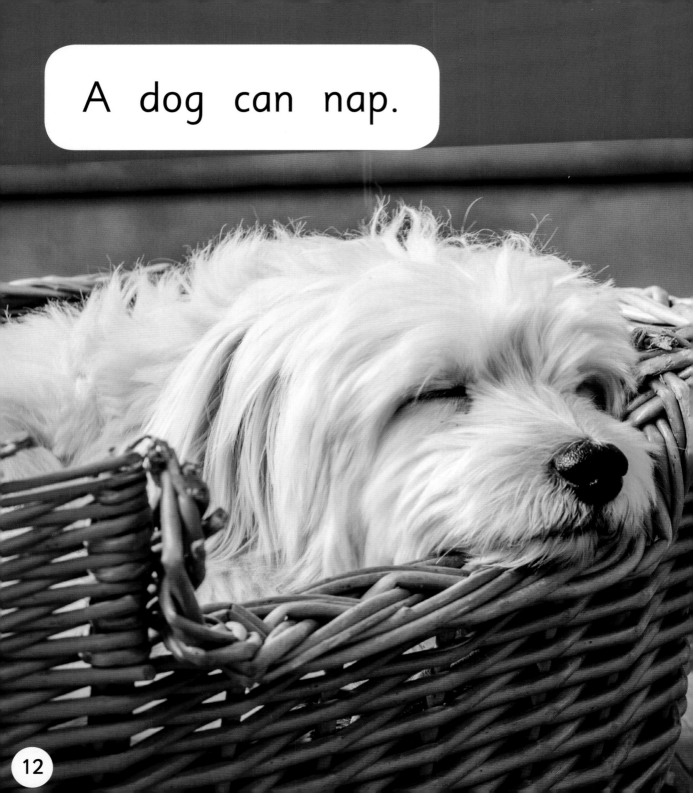

A dog can nap.